# Reptile Keeper's Guides

# BOX
# TURTLES

### R. D. Bartlett
### Patricia Bartlett

D1732718

BARRON'S

## Acknowledgments

Many people have helped us in creating this book. We especially appreciate the expertise and kindnesses of Rob MacInnes and Mike Stuhlman of Glades Herp, Inc., Randy Babb of the Arizona Game and Fish Department, Eric Thiss of ZooBooks, Chris McQuade of Gulf Coast Reptiles; Ron and Adrian Bird, Tom Davis, Kenny Wray, Buzz Ross, Carl May, Don Hamper, Jim Harding, Pete Wilson, and Scott Pfaff. We'd also like to thank the many hobbyists we have met, some in out-of-the-way places, who have shared their knowledge and questions with us. To Laurel Robinson and our editor, Anna Damaskos, our special thanks.

*All inquiries should be addressed to:*
Barron's Educational Series, Inc.
250 Wireless Boulevard
Hauppauge, NY 11788
**http://www.barronseduc.com**

*Library of Congress Catalog Card No. 2001029515*

ISBN-13: 978-0-7641-1701-5
ISBN-10: 0-7641-1701-7

**Library of Congress Cataloging-in-Publication Data**
Bartlett, Richard D., 1938–
    Box turtles / R.D. Bartlett and Patricia Bartlett.
        p.   cm. — (Reptile keeper's guides)
    ISBN 0-7641-1701-7
        1. Box turtles as pets. I. Bartlett, Patricia Pope,
    1949–  II. Title.
SF459.T8 B368 2001
639.3'925–dc21                              2001029515

Printed in China
9 8 7 6 5 4

# Contents

# Preface

Many of us remember our first encounters with a box turtle. For me (Patti) it was riding in the family car with my parents on one of our biennial journeys to see relatives in Georgia. The first day of the trip was bound to be boring, but the second and third days weren't bad. Those were the days when the sight of a box turtle crossing the road was a reason for celebration. And once in a while on the return trip, my parents would yield to the frenzied shrieks of four children under the age of ten to "Stop! *Stop!* We want a turtle!" They'd pull the aged station wagon to the side of the road and pick up a box turtle. We never knew that there were different kinds of box turtles—I think I just thought they were different ages and maybe different sexes. We'd take the turtle home with us and turn it loose in our backyard. Once in a while, we'd find one chomping down a fallen peach or apple from the trees in the yard. It wasn't until much later that I learned that there were many kinds of box turtles, some strikingly bold with yellow lines on black, others with brown-splotched shells that looked like finely inlaid boxes.

Today there are more roads between Albuquerque and Atlanta, and fewer box turtles crossing them. But these gentle creatures with the perceptive gaze still have the ability to make even the staunchest turtle nonfancier pause and think, "Well, now, that's a pretty little thing. . . ." We hope this book will introduce these creatures to a new generation of pet keepers who will find them worthy of protection and herpetoculture.

Dick and Patti Bartlett
Gainesville, Florida, USA

Despite being encumbered by a heavy shell, many box turtles go up and over rather than around an object. This is a male eastern box turtle, *Terrapene c. carolina*.

2

# Introduction

Simply stated, box turtles as a group are not brilliantly colored. Of those that do boast bright colors, however, the brightest is from the eastern United States. This is the eastern box turtle, *Terrapene carolina*. Some eastern box turtle males—the brighter of the sexes—are a wonderful combination of orange or yellow on brown.

Other races of the eastern box turtle are darker, with the big Gulf Coast race being darkest and largest. Though dark, the Florida box turtle has an interesting pattern of thin yellow radiating marks on each carapacial scute. This is echoed, but in a coarser form, by the more westerly ornate box turtle.

None of the Asian box turtles have radiating carapacial marks, and only one, the Indochinese box turtle, could be considered prettily marked. As a matter of fact, the markings of some Indochinese box turtles are so intricate that one native name—the hundred-flower—seems somehow appropriate.

Because no box turtles are bred extensively in captivity, no aberrant colors have yet been established. A very few albino specimens of the ornate and eastern box turtle have been reported. Additionally, and more recently, a few hatchling eastern box turtles of unusually light color (see photo, page 4) have been found.

Box turtles of all species were once common, easily found, readily available to hobbyists, and inexpensive. Today, all forms are far less common, a few are virtually unobtainable, and some are remarkably expensive. Prices run the gamut from $25 for an ornate box turtle (readily available) to $1,500 for a Chinese three-striped box turtle (seldom available).

At a shell length of 8 to 8.5 inches (20 to 21 cm) when adult, male Gulf Coast box turtles, *Terrapene carolina major,* are the largest of the American forms.

Aberrant colorations, such as shown on this hypomelanistic hatchling eastern box turtle, *Terrapene c. carolina,* are well documented.

These ornate box turtles, *Terrapene o. ornata,* were walking along a Texas roadside.

The box turtles of eastern North America range widely through woodland habitats, as well as overgrown fields and meadows, and wet prairies. Those of western North America (including most Mexican forms) appear in drier habitats, being creatures of grasslands, prairies, and even deserts. The aquatic box turtle of north central Mexico is an exception, being restricted to a small area of marshland. The Asian forms wander through wooded and open lands, and several appear in rice paddies and other shallow water situations. Some are associated with mountain streams and other water sources.

Population reductions have been caused by numerous factors. The habitat of American box turtles has been reduced and fragmented. The turtles were long sold in the pet market, are among the most popular and coveted of pet turtles, and, sadly, are often run over as they attempt to cross one of the roadways that invariably transect the remaining box turtle habitat.

Pressures on the Asian box turtles have been a little different, but no less detrimental. These turtles are staples in the diet and medicinal markets of many Asian cultures, and that market is huge. Second to actual consumption (in one form or another) is collection for the pet trade.

According to species, box turtles may vary from being primarily terrestrial to being essentially aquatic. Most of these turtles are diurnal, and all are especially active. All have a strong transverse hinge on the plastron, and all can draw both halves of the plastron upward against the bottom of the carapace. This tight closure of the shells gives the common name of "box" turtle. The tight closure offers the box turtles more protection from predators than is afforded by the nonmovable shells of many other species.

The plastral hinge is undeveloped at the time of hatching, but develops and strengthens with age and growth.

There is not a great diversity in size among the box turtles. The adults of all are commonly between 5.5 and 7.5 inches (13 and 19 cm) in shell length (rarely larger). Many are highly domed, whereas some are more streamlined in appearance.

Box turtles are quite omnivorous, consuming not only vegetation such as fruits, leaves, and mushrooms, but also avidly seeking and eating insects, worms, mollusks, and carrion.

Baby box turtles of all of the species are very secretive, and are most often associated with habitats somewhat damper than those needed by the adults.

Although turtles are often thought of as solitary creatures, areas of ideal habitats can house fairly large

Male Indochinese box turtles, *Cuora (Cistoclemmys) galbinifrons,* often have all-yellow heads.

populations that randomly, or deliberately, come into contact with one another.

We retain a number of box turtles (some have been with us for decades) of several species. All are housed communally in a large outside pen, and their interactions can be complex. In captivity, as in the wild, occasional male-to-male territorial disputes may flare, but are usually resolved quickly. Sometimes the weaker or smaller turtle is overturned and the upright turtle is the winner. In a hard packed pen, the loser can easily right himself and

The plastral hinge is undeveloped and the egg sac usually large at hatching. This is a Florida box turtle, *Terrapene carolina bauri.*

Three kinds of box turtles have joined the large radiated tortoises for a vegetable repast.

This is an adult Chinese box turtle, *Cuora (Cistoclemmys) flavomarginata.*

Many eastern box turtles, *Terrapene c. carolina,* have brightly marked head and legs, but a dark carapace.

depart, but he usually waits until the winning turtle leaves. Sometimes the turtles will butt their shells into each other until the weaker or smaller turtle turns around and hurries off.

Ours are fed a wide variety of animate (earthworms and insects) and inanimate (dark green leafy lettuces

Hatchling Florida box turtles, *Terrapene carolina bauri,* usually have a yellow vertebral stripe.

and berries) items, which are occasionally enhanced with a dusting of multivitamins and calcium. The adults mate and the females nest, and the eggs are left to incubate in the ground. The fast-growing hatchlings, which we find in the pen each summer and autumn, are often brought indoors to be given a head start before being put back with the adults. They are given weekly dietary supplements of D3 and calcium and daily exposure to full-spectrum lighting. Under such a regimen, growth is rapid, and the babies are ready for outdoor life in about a year's time.

We fully understand the infatuation that some folks have with these interesting and hardy turtles, and hope that the information that we have provided herein will help you— whether you are a new hobbyist or a longtime enthusiast—better understand your box turtle.

# What Is a Box Turtle?

To most reptile hobbyists, a box turtle is a turtle of virtually any species that has a hinged and closable plastron. Using that criterion, box turtles are found in North America and in Asia/Indochina. In America the box turtles are among the most recognizable of the turtles, or chelonians. There are four North American species, three with subspecies. The box turtles and the Blanding's turtles are American turtles having a hinged plastron. In Asia/Indochina there are several turtle species (or "box turtles") with strongly hinged plastrons as well. At least of these two, Asian/Indochinese species are rather extensively aquatic.

Despite their terrestrial propensities, the box turtles are closely allied to many aquatic forms. The American species are in the family Emydidae and the subfamily Emydinae. The Asian box turtles were in the family Emydidae, subfamily Batugurinae. This subfamily has recently been elevated to full family status, which split the box turtles into two families—the North America box turtles into Emydidae and the Asian box turtles into Batuguridae.

All of the North American box turtles have highly domed carapaces (top shells). In the east, these turtles dwell in woodlands and wet prairies. In the west and Mexico (with the exception of the aquatic box turtle of Cuatro Cienegas, Sonora), they dwell in dry prairies and even in desert grasslands.

Several of the Asian box turtles, *Cuora* with 11 species (3 of which may be referred to the genus *Cistoclemmys* by some authorities) and *Pyxidea* with 1 species, also have highly domed shells, but other Asian box turtles are of more streamlined appearance. As currently understood, despite considerable geographic variation within some species, none are subspeciated.

Note the diversity in the plastral markings of these ornate box turtles, *Terrapene o. ornata*.

## The American and Asian Box Turtles

| Common name | Scientific name | Principal range | Size in inches (cm) |
| --- | --- | --- | --- |
| **Eastern box turtles** | | | |
| Florida box turtle | *Terrapene carolina bauri* | Florida | 6.5 (16) |
| Eastern box turtle | *T. c. carolina* | Northeastern USA | 6.5 (16) |
| Gulf Coast box turtle | *T. c. major* | Eastern Gulf Coast | 8 (20) |
| Mexican box turtle | *T. c. mexicana* | Tamaulipas, San Luis Potosi, and Vera Cruz, Mexico | 5.5 (13) |
| Three-toed box turtle | *T. c. triunguis* | plains states, USA | 7 (18) |
| Yucatan box turtle | *T. c. yucatana* | Yucatan Peninsula, Mexico | 6.5 (16) |
| **Aquatic box turtle** | | | |
| Aquatic box turtle | *Terrapene coahuila* | Coahuila, Mexico | 6 (15) |
| **Spotted box turtles** | | | |
| Klauber's box turtle | *Terrapene nelsoni klauberi* | Southwestern Sonora and adjacent Sinaloa, Mexico | 5.5 (13) |
| Spotted box turtle | *Terrapene n. nelsoni* | Nyarit, Mexico | 5.5 (13) |

The ability to close the plastron (bottom shell) is well developed in all adult box turtles. The cartilaginous hinge is in the suture between the pectoral and abdominal scales of the plastron. The hinge is entirely undeveloped at hatching, but develops as the turtle grows. By the time a box turtle is about one-quarter grown, the plastron can be drawn tightly against the edge of the carapace. Or at least it can be closed tightly during the lean times in the turtle's life. However, when worms and grasshoppers are abundant and the berry season is in full swing, box turtles may become so corpulent that they are unable to close their plastron. When the shells are closed up tightly, they protect the turtle from predators such as small mammals. Alas, the shells provide no protection against introduced predators such as fire ants.

| Common name | Scientific name | Principal range | Size in inches (cm) |
|---|---|---|---|
| **Western box turtles** | | | |
| Desert box turtle | *Terrapene ornata luteola* | Southern New Mexico, southeastern Arizona, adjacent Mexico | 5 (12) |
| Ornate box turtle | *T. o. ornata* | plains states, USA | 6 (15) |
| **Asian box turtles** | | | |
| Yellow-margined box turtle | *Cuora (Cistoclemmys) flavomarginata* | Southern China and Ryukyu Islands | 7 (18) |
| Indochinese box turtle | *Cuora (Cistoclemmys) galbinifrons* | Vietnam and Hainan Island, China | 7 (18) |
| McCord's box turtle | *Cuora (Cistoclemmys) mccordi* | Kwangsi, China | 5 (12) |
| Malayan box turtle | *Cuora amboinensis* | Southeast Asia and Malaya | 8 (20) |
| Yellow-headed box turtle | *Cuora aurocapitata* | Anhui, China | 5 (12) |
| Yunnan green box turtle | *Cuora chriskarannarum* | Yunnan Province, China | 6 (15) |
| Hainan box turtle | *Cuora hainanensis* | Hainan Island, China | 7 (18) |
| Pan's box turtle | *Cuora pani* | Shaanxi Province, China | 6 (15) |
| Chinese three-striped box turtle | *Cuora trifasciata* | Northern Vietnam and southern China | 8 (20) |
| Yunnan box turtle | *Cuora yunnanensis* | Yunnan Province, China | 5 (12) |
| Zhou's box turtle | *Cuora zhoui* | Guangxi and Yunnan, China | 5 (12) |
| Keeled box turtle | *Pyxidea mouhoti* | Hainan Island, China, and Vietnam | 6.5 (16) |

All box turtles feed opportunistically. Although they eat a wide variety of plant material (berries and other fruits, some greens, and many mushrooms), they always seem more eager to feed on snails, slugs, worms, insects, and carrion. Captives eat all of these things plus a wide variety of prepared foods.

However, like two-year-old humans who want to eat only macaroni and cheese, some captives will choose a particular food item and steadfastly refuse other offerings. Although it can be difficult, you should immediately dissuade the turtle from this practice and train it to accept a wide spectrum of food.

Despite their wide latitude of dietary and habitat preferences, box turtles are not always the easiest of chelonians to acclimate to captive conditions. Some may eat well at first, then languish for no apparent reason.

This is the Asian species, *Pyxidea mouhoti,* dull in color but alert in demeanor.

Chinese three-striped box turtles, *Cuora trifasciata* are alert and very shy.

Some may never feed when removed from the wild, but many thrive. And those that do thrive may live for more than half a century, and perhaps even push a century for their total life span.

Humidity-loving Asian and eastern North American box turtles can be especially difficult to acclimate in our arid western states, and vice versa: arid-adapted western and three-toed box turtles often do poorly in the humid East or in foggy regions of the West.

To accurately sex box turtles, check the secondary sexual characteristics. Certain of these characteristics may vary subspecifically.

• Tail shape. The tail of adult male box turtles is thicker and somewhat longer than that of the female. This holds true for all species and subspecies.
• Plastron shape. Adult males of some species and subspecies have a plastral concavity in the rear lobe of the plastron. This concavity may or may not

Note the red eyes and hooked beak of this adult male eastern box turtle, *Terrapene c. carolina.*

This is the typical plastron color of the Chinese three-striped box turtle, *Cuora trifasciata.*

Note the plastral hinge that allows the box turtle to close its shell tightly. The concavity in the rear lobe indicates that this eastern box turtle, *Terrapene c. carolina,* is a male.

Many box turtles lose their lives to vehicles. Carl May photographed this white-faced male Gulf Coast box turtle, *Terrapene carolina major,* as it was about to cross a road.

be present on male three-toed box turtles, and is often only vaguely discernible in Asiatic species. This concavity makes it easier for the male box turtle to stay atop the female when they breed.

- Eye color. Adult males of the ornate, desert, eastern, and Gulf Coast box turtles often have red irises (sometimes brownish); those of the females are usually yellow or brown, but may occasionally be a dull red. The irises of male three-toed box turtles may be reddish, but often aren't. There is no sexually related color difference in the eyes of the Florida box turtle or in Asian species.
- Hind feet. Males of the American box turtles tend to have curved, hooklike claws on their hind feet. The innermost toe of the ornate and desert box turtles can be rotated inward.

A quick review of the "pet" status of several species of box turtle will give you a basic understanding of what's readily available and what has been protected.

The various races of the eastern box turtle are protected by law in many of the states in which they appear. Unfortunately, this "paper protection" does not address or correct other very real pressures upon the populations. These include loss of suitable habitat (including habitat fragmentation), vehicular deaths as the creatures cross highways, and

Natural causes claim the lives of many box turtles. This shell of the Gulf Coast box turtle, *Terrapene carolina major,* was found in a wooded area of the Florida Panhandle.

*Cuora pani,* Pan's box turtle, is similar to but duller, and apparently more uncommon, than the Chinese three-striped box turtle.

This male Mexican box turtle, *Terrapene carolina mexicana,* is in the collection of the Gladys Porter Zoo, Brownsville, TX.

casual collecting by individuals for pets. Increased predation, especially on the eggs and hatchlings, by a burgeoning number of predators (fire ants, raccoons, opossums, armadillos, foxes, and domestic dogs among them) is another pressure that continues to cause population declines.

Because it is on the federal endangered species list, the aquatic box turtle, *Terrapene coahuila,* is virtually never seen in the pet trade.

The western box turtles are not as rigidly protected and remain readily available to hobbyists.

Although questions exist about the continued well-being of American box turtle populations, the status of the Asian box turtles is even more poorly understood. Many Asian cultures consider these small and innocuous turtles dietary delicacies, and hundred of thousands are collected and brought to food markets annually. The "Shall I sell it or shall I eat it?" question has affected prices for the pet Asian box turtles. The prices for Asian box turtles continue to climb, with the Chinese three-striped box turtle, *Cuora trifasciata,* being particularly expensive. Young adults of this species are now (early 2001) commanding $1,500 each.

# The New World or American Box Turtles

There are only four species of box turtles in North America, and only two of these occur in the United States. In the United States, the eastern box turtle, *Terrapene carolina* ssp., has four subspecies and the western box turtle, *T. ornata* ssp., has two.

The eastern box turtle has two additional races in Mexico. The Mexican forms, *T. carolina yucatana* and *T. c. mexicana,* are not available in the pet trade.

The two races of the third species, *T. nelsoni,* are restricted in distribution to Mexico. These are virtually unknown in the pet trade.

In these pages we will discuss the four subspecies of eastern box turtles that occur in the United States. These are the eastern box turtle, *T. c. carolina;* the Florida box turtle, *T. c. bauri;* the Gulf Coast box turtle, *T. c. major;* and the three-toed box turtle, *T. c. triunguis.* These are the ones most often kept as pets.

Of these four subspecies, the eastern box turtle occupies the largest range. Many specimens are prettily colored in yellows, oranges, and warm browns, but others are quite drab. This highly domed, oval turtle is found from northern Florida to Massachusetts and from Michigan to northwestern Mississippi. It is a meadow edge and open woodland species. It usually has four toes on the hind feet. Although it is often found near pond and lake edges as well as along woodland and damp meadow streams, the eastern box turtle seldom enters water more than an inch or two in depth. If it is forced into or accidentally topples into deep water, it usually bobs on the surface like a cork while paddling clumsily toward the nearest shore.

The Florida box turtle is entirely unlike its more northerly cousin in both appearance and color. The carapace is black (or nearly black), elongate, and marked with well-delineated radiations of yellow. The rear of the carapace flares outward. The proportionately narrow carapace is very highly domed. There are two yellow lines (these are sometimes fragmented) on each side of the head. This race, which for all intents and purposes is endemic to Florida, cannot be legally commercialized. Damp, open woodlands, damp meadows, marshes, and swamp edges are favored habitats. This species can swim, but seldom voluntarily does so.

In contrast, the Gulf Coast box turtle often enters water and may be seen walking along the bottom of rather deep canals and water holes of various kinds. It is the largest of the four subspecies and, although highly domed, has the carapace rather flattened centrally. The posterior marginals of the males flare widely. This big box turtle has a dull brownish-black carapace upon which light markings are often vaguely discernible. Old males often have facial markings consisting of a chalk-white mustache or mustache and sideburns. In its pure, non-intergraded form, the Gulf Coast box turtle occurs only on Florida's Panhandle. However, intergrade specimens ("hybrids" between two neighboring subspecies) showing much Gulf Coast box turtle influence may be encountered from eastern Louisiana to central Georgia. Look for this turtle in moist woodlands and along marsh edges.

The three-toed box turtle is the most westerly race of the eastern box turtle. Although it inhabits open woodlands, it also ranges far into grassland and prairie habitats. Look for it from Missouri and Alabama to eastern Texas and Kansas. Although

The red eyes of this Gulf Coast box turtle, *Terrapene carolina major,* indicate that it is an adult male.

some specimens may be rather brightly colored, many show a tendency toward a unicolored olive-brown, olive-tan, or tannish-brown carapace. Adult males may have a fair amount of red or maroon on the head.

The range of the pretty ornate box turtle, one of the two western box turtles, overlaps the range of the three-toed box turtle in the eastern plains states. The ornate box turtles can be especially difficult captives in humid areas, refusing most foods and languishing until death.

Although the ornate box turtle and the Florida box turtle look superficially similar, the two are actually easily differentiated. The dark carapace of the ornate box turtle is highly domed but is flattened centrally. The carapace of the Florida box turtle is highly domed and peaked centrally. Additionally, the prominent, radiating yellow carapacial lines are thick and less precisely delineated than those of the Florida box turtle. The ornate box turtle has a spotted head; the head of the Florida box turtle is striped. The ornate box turtle has a dark plastron that is heavily streaked with bold light lines; the plastron of the Florida box

turtle is light, occasionally with a few dark markings.

The desert box turtle, *T. o. luteola*, is like a pale, more busily patterned ornate box turtle. Its carapacial markings are thinner, more numerous, and usually do not contrast sharply with the ground color. All markings are best defined on young specimens; old specimens may be an almost unicolored yellowish-tan or tannish brown. The desert box turtle may be found from far western Texas, westward to eastern Arizona, and southward across the Rio Grande into adjacent Mexico.

Male western box turtles have the innermost toe enlarged and angled differently from the others. This helps them during breeding in positioning themselves atop the female.

Both the ornate and the desert box turtles are creatures of open plains, prairies, deserts, and related scrub and low-brush thickets. Despite this, they are often most common near stock tanks, in irrigated areas, and along the edges of water holes and river edges. *T. o. ornata* appears in patches of suitable habitat from Indiana and South Dakota to the lower Rio Grande Valley.

The Florida box turtle, *Terrapene carolina bauri,* has a narrow and highly domed carapace.

# The Old World Box Turtles

Of the 12 species of Asian and Malayan box turtles, only 5 are seen with any regularity in the pet trade. Of these five, two, the very aquatic Malayan box turtle and the essentially terrestrial Chinese box turtle, are the most commonly available. Of the remaining three species, the Indochinese box turtle and the keeled box turtle are both primarily terres-

Even when patterned (such as the example on the left) three-toed box turtles, *Terrapene carolina truinguis,* are not brightly colored.

trial, and the very expensive Chinese three-striped box turtle is aquatic.

The most inexpensive ($25–$40) of the Asian box turtles is *Cuora amboinensis.* Despite a range extending well beyond the confines of Malaya, this species is frequently referred to as the Malayan box turtle. In additional to being found in Malaya, it is found from the Philippines to the Nicobars, and from Vietnam through Thailand. It is one of the most aquatic and least colorful of the genus, yet it is attractive. The smoothly rounded carapace of an adult varies, by population, from somewhat flattened to highly domed, and is black in coloration. The plastron is yellowish, as are the areas where the limbs and head join the body (called the soft body parts). The limbs are dark. The dark head and neck are prominently striped with yellow. The uppermost pair of stripes (one on each side) converge on the tip of the snout. The hatchlings are dark and have three dorsal keels (tricarinate). This is a rather slow-moving, shy turtle. Imports are quick to withdraw into the safety of their shells and may remain immobile and withdrawn for periods upward of an hour. Although most are considerably smaller, the Malayan box turtle does occasionally attain a shell length of 8 inches.

The most popular of the Asian box turtles with hobbyists is *Cuora flavomarginata,* the Chinese box turtle. Most specimens available in the pet trade are wild-collected and imported from China. A very few are now being captive-bred. Determined by availability, the price of this species fluctuates wildly. Because of a decreased availability, the price of this pretty turtle is continuing to climb. At a recent herp expo (August 2000) captive-bred hatchlings were selling for $125 to $175, and wild-collected adults were being offered for $250 each. This species swims rather well, but also thrives in terrestrial situations.

The shell of the Chinese box turtle is moderately to highly domed, and the concentric growth rings remain prominent (unless physically worn from the shell by abrasion). The carapacial color of the yellow-rimmed box turtle is somewhat variable, being brown, olive-brown, or black. There is usually a rather prominent yellow vertebral stripe, and the marginals, the scutes edging the upper shell, are yellow on their undersides. It is this yellow rim from which both common and specific names are derived. The head is very prettily colored. The olive-gray to olive-brown of the crown is separated from the yellow-green of the cheeks by a yellow (sometimes

The center of the carapace of an adult ornate box turtle, *Terrapene o. ornata,* is flattened.

greenish yellow) stripe that is thinly delineated by a darker edging. The lower cheeks and chin shade to a pale peach to brighter yellow. The legs are dark and where they join the body, the axilla, are yellowish. This turtle can be very difficult to sex accurately. The tail of *both* sexes is short, but that of the male is comparatively wider at the base. Chinese box turtles breed both in the water and on land.

The Indochinese box turtle, *Cuora galbinifrons,* is (arguably) the most beautifully colored of the Old World box turtles. It is also the most difficult to acclimate to captive conditions. When first imported, these turtles cost several hundred dollars each. They are now selling at less than $100. An idea of the beauty of this turtle is indicated by an alternative American name of "hundred-flower turtle." This seems a literal translation of one of several Vietnamese names applied to the species. Many dealers continue to list *C. galbinifrons* as the "three-hill box turtle," a reference to geographic origin.

The Indochinese box turtle is an interesting and intricate combination of buff (or tan) and brown. There is often a buff vertebral stripe dividing

the brown, but for this species, a picture of the carapacial pattern actually is worth the proverbial thousand words. The head, neck, and limbs are tan(ish). The head may be reticulated or flecked with darker pigment. Adults range from 6.5 to 8 inches (16 to 20 cm) in carapace length. This terrestrial turtle is known to dwell in high-elevation woodlands in Vietnam and surrounding areas.

Another Chinese three-striped box turtle, *Cuora trifasciata,* is still occasionally seen in the pet trade. It is highly aquatic and has a low-domed and elongate carapace. The current price for this species (year 2000) is $1,500 each. The three-keeled carapace of this turtle varies from brown to terra-cotta. A dark stripe is present on each keel.

The keeled box turtle, *Pyxidea mouhoti,* is an interesting if quietly colored turtle species. The carapace is of some shade of brown and has two keels, one near the top of each row of costal plates.

There is nothing colorful about keeled box turtles. Head, limbs, tail, and carapace are rather uniformly hued in some shade of brown. It may stray toward tan on some specimens or toward russet on others, but there is always a brown overtone.

The plastron, also brown, usually bears a dark smudge in each scute. The plastron is smaller than the bottom of the carapace, and thus does not fully conceal the turtle when it is closed. The flattened middorsal area and flattened slanting costal scutes gives the keeled box turtle a characteristic shape. The alternative common name of jagged-shelled turtle comes from the jaggedly serrate posterior edge of the carapace.

# Box Turtles as Pets

## Choosing a Healthy Turtle or Tortoise

What kind of box turtle should you get?

Many pet box turtles are picked up from the wild by individuals on camping trips, hikes, or while fishing or hunting. Other box turtles may wander into suburban and rural gardens, and are found and saved by a kind-hearted person from vehicular turtlecide as the turtles venture onto a roadway. Some may be acquired from friends or from other sources.

Asian box turtles are not protected in America. However, some of the North American forms are offered some degree of protection by many states. Thus, no matter where you acquire your box turtle, it is a good idea to be aware of any laws that may pertain to your pet.

It may be necessary to acquire a permit merely to keep any form of eastern box turtle in several of the New England states, and it is illegal to purchase or sell one in many other states. Some states may allow you to keep only a specific number. In Florida, for example, a maximum of two eastern box turtles of any race can be kept without a license by each person in a household, and the turtles cannot be bought and sold for profit.

The states of Iowa and Wisconsin protect the ornate box turtle.

Mexico forbids the removal of any box turtle from that country without a permit. The aquatic box turtle (also of Mexico) is an endangered species. You must have a permit to collect one from the wild, or to sell or barter for one in interstate commerce.

The laws can be complex, but you must learn and abide by them.

The adult aquatic box turtle, *Terrapene coahuila,* is long, low, and dull in color. It is on the federal endangered species list.

# Behavior Clues and General Health

Box turtles are well known for their habit of withdrawing into their shells closing the plastron, and remaining there for upward of an hour. Wild specimens are more apt to do this than captive-bred ones. Even when they begin to open, it is often a lengthy process. First the plastron is lowered a little, then after a while it is lowered a little more, and finally it is relaxed entirely. Even then, though, the tail, limbs, and head will remain fully withdrawn. Just when you are about to give up, a nose will appear, and a few minutes later an eye. Then the turtle will wait again. To say this is exasperating if you are trying to assess health is an understatement—especially if you inadvertently move a little and the turtle withdraws and closes again, and both of you have to start the whole process over.

But eventually the box turtle will open its shell, extend its head, neck, and limbs, and take a few steps, giving you at least a fleeting chance to look it over.

What should you look for when considering the purchase of a box turtle? How does the appearance of a healthy specimen differ from that of one that is ill?

All things, including the agility with which the animal withdraws into its shell as well as the persistence with which it remains hidden, must be considered when choosing a turtle or tortoise. And there *are* a couple of things you can consider even when the turtle has withdrawn, and there's a nonthreatening trick or two that you can use to induce the box turtle to cooperate.

First of all, slowly approach the specimen in which you are interested. To a chelonian that is already frightened by capture and caging, any large approaching shape means danger, and a fast-moving large shape is usually considered more dangerous than a slow-moving or stationary one. If you move slowly, you may find that you are able to approach rather closely without inducing a complete withdrawal by the specimen. Once touched, a frightened

Klauber's box turtle, *Terrapene nelsoni klauberi,* is a seldom-seen Mexican species.

This subadult Chinese box turtle, *Cuora (Cistoclemmys) flavomarginata,* is foraging for seeds and insects.

As box turtles often do, this three-toed adult *(Terrapene carolina triunguis)* is quietly surveying his domain.

turtle will remain withdrawn longer than one that has not been touched. And yes, a turtle *can* feel its shell being touched, just as you can feel your fingernail being touched.

Your box turtle must have eyes that are bright and clear. The turtle's eyes should have neither exudate nor encrustations around or beneath them, nor should its lids be puffy and swollen. The box turtle should also follow your movements with its eyes.

There should be no bubbling or wheezing from the nostrils, even when the head is quickly withdrawn. Either or both of these manifestations probably indicate the presence of a respiratory ailment. The box turtle should be breathing normally through its nostrils with mouth closed.

Unless your box turtle is a hatchling (when its shell will be a little soft) its shell should be firm and nonpliable, and the turtle should have a heavy, solid feel.

All limbs should be fully functional and not swollen.

Advanced problems can vary from difficult to impossible to correct.

Red, white, and black markings often adorn the face of male three-toed box turtles, *Terrapene carolina triunguis*. Females are less brightly colored.

If these are present, do not purchase the specimen.

Some box turtles, at some point in their life, may experience the trauma of a broken shell or severe burns (perhaps from a forest or grassland fire). If the cracks or breaks have healed satisfactorily (resulting only in cosmetic disfigurement once completely healed), or the burned shell has lost only a few scutes, this is merely a cosmetic problem. If the animal is otherwise healthy and you do not mind the less-than-perfect appearance, there is no reason you should not purchase the turtle.

Ask to see your potential purchase eat. Although most healthy turtles have fine appetites, a very few specimens may outwardly appear healthy but refuse to feed. The causes for this lack of a feeding response can be varied. The turtle may be ill, or it may not have had food offered for an extended period of time. It may have been offered an incorrect diet.

This is a portrait of the yellow-headed box turtle, *Cuora aurocapitata.*

This male three-toed box turtle, *Terrapene carolina triunguis,* was photographed on a roadside in east Texas.

Athough the American box turtles and many of their Asian counterparts feed when out of water, others, such as the Malayan and Chinese three-striped box turtles, often prefer to eat while in the water.

You must keep in mind the fact that box turtles are naturally shy, and simply may not eat while you are watching. If the turtle feels heavy and looks healthy otherwise, it still may be perfectly safe to purchase it. However, if the turtle does not have good body weight and you do not see it eat, you might want to rethink your intentions of buying it.

There is, of course, a chance that once you get your box turtle home you will notice a problem that was not apparent at the store. You should immediately notify the vendor of the turtle, but in many cases all animal sales are final. Box turtles are very slow to show external manifestations of any health problem (other than a physical injury). Because of this, if you notice a health problem severe enough to cause you concern, we urge you to consult your veterinarian.

Always remember that box turtles can carry salmonella. Wash your hands before and after handling your box turtles. You don't want to pass on any pathogen to your box turtle, either.

This Gulf Coast box turtle, *Terrapene carolina major,* was scarred by fire. Photo by Carl May.

# Where Should You Get Your Box Turtle?

Box turtles are available from numerous sources. You may choose to collect your own from the wild. Before doing so, check your state's game and nongame laws to ascertain whether collecting a box turtle is legal in your state or province.

Many pet shops carry the more commonly available kinds of box turtles (especially ornate box turtles). If you choose this avenue of acquisition and are not an experienced hobbyist, bring a knowledgeable person with you to help you assess the overall health of the specimen in which you are interested.

Specialty reptile dealers and breeders of box turtles advertise regularly in the classified sections of hobbyist-oriented reptile and amphibian magazines and on the Web. Most advertisers are honest and try hard to supply healthy specimens of high quality; some are unscrupulous. Check out the reliability of a given company or person with fellow hobbyists. Because in most cases you will be purchasing the specimen sight unseen, it is a case of buyer beware. Ask pertinent and pointed

Indochinese box turtles, *Cuora (Cistoclemmys) galbinifrons,* like this adult male, are collected from the wild for the pet trade.

questions about the appearance, health, and general hardiness of the specimen and species in question. Be aware that shipping charges (including COD fees if applicable) significantly increase the purchase price.

Do not expect every specimen, especially wild-collected ones, to look picture-book perfect. Some races of the eastern box turtle may vary widely in ground color and markings. The time to ask questions is *before* the purchase, not after. Good luck!

This *Cuora pani,* Pan's box turtle, was photographed at the Riverbanks Zoo in Columbia, SC.

# Caging

Conventional wisdom has it that box turtles are among the most ideal of "pet" turtles. And they *are* great, but not until *after* they have been acclimated to captive conditions.

Adult box turtles may be housed either indoors or outside, but they are better suited for the latter, at least during nice weather. The health and habits of babies are more easily monitored when the turtles are kept indoors.

When content and secure, box turtles are relatively active, coursing as widely as cage constraints will allow. Box turtles are walkers. If insecure (such as when freshly collected from the wild or if cage temperatures are incorrect), the turtles may sit for days on end, drawn morosely into their shells, awaiting better conditions.

If kept indoors, box turtles need a large enclosure. We suggest a minimum floor space of 2 by 4 feet (60 by 121 cm), the size of the bottom of a 75-gallon (285-l) aquarium, be provided for a pair or a trio of adult box turtles. A cage of 4 by 8 feet (121 by 242 cm), the size of a sheet of plywood, is actually preferable. Box turtles can climb, but are not particularly agile. Depending on the depth of the substrate that you intend on maintaining in the cage, walls of 12 to 15 inches (30 to 38 cm), preferably with a small overhang, will suffice.

Besides a sizable land area, species such as the Malayan box turtle and the Chinese three-striped box turtle will require a water receptacle large enough to submerge and move about in. If you hope to breed them, the water receptacle will need to be at least 12 by 30 inches (30 by 76 cm) and about a foot deep in the deepest part. The water will need frequent cleaning.

A number of different substrates may be used in indoor cages. Newspaper is readily available, absorbent, and easily changed, but

This small plastic feeding tub holds juveniles of several kinds of box turtles and a pair of baby Asian four-eyed turtles.

Note that this Malayan box turtle, *Cuora amboinensis,* lacks any pinkish color on the carapace.

its smooth surface does not give the box turtles much purchase. Rolled corrugate is absorbent and provides the turtles with more certain footing. Indoor-outdoor carpeting also provides a secure walking surface and can be washed or discarded when it becomes dirty. Pelletized alfalfa is dry, inexpensive, provides traction, and is digestible if it's accidentally ingested while the box turtle is feeding. However, since it absorbs both moisture and contaminants, the condition of the alfalfa pellets must be carefully monitored. Scoop out the damp or soiled portions—they will quickly mold and create conditions that are unfavorable for turtles and humans alike. Nonaromatic mulches or dried leaves may also be used as substrate for box turtles. This provides good footing and is absorbent. At times box turtles can act much like small bulldozers and completely rearrange their cage decor.

# Light and Heat

Indoor cages will require both lighting and heating. Captive box turtles often awaken and actively forage during the brightest (but not necessarily the hottest) parts of the day. Unless you intend on hibernating your box turtles (Asian, Gulf Coast, Florida, and southernmost individuals of other species and subspecies will require no period

of hibernation), combined light and heat is especially important during the cooler months. Depending on its area of origin, a box turtle will be most comfortable when kept from 75 to 85°F (23.3 to 29.4°C), with a hotter spot for basking.

Your box turtle's cage can be heated with overhead lighting (our preference), by using a heating pad underneath the cage, or by a combination of both.

Undertank heaters (specially made heating pads) for use with terrariums are commercially available.

A brilliantly illuminated basking and feeding area will be appreciated by your box turtles. The source of the lighting does not have to be particularly sophisticated. Clamp on reflectors with 75-watt incandescent bulbs. These are suspended 12 to 18 inches (30 to 45 cm) above the feeding-basking area. The temperature on the basking area should be about 88–94°F (31.3–35.2°C).

Incandescent lights do not provide the ultraviolet waves so beneficial to your box turtles. However, a newly available bulb, billed as a UV-B/heat bulb, does provide a fair quantity of

Some eastern box turtles, *Terrapene c. carolina,* are very brightly colored.

The yellow temporal stripe and pink cheeks are typical of the Chinese box turtle, *Cuora (Cistoclemmys) flavomarginata.*

the beneficial UV-B waves. Some fluorescent tubes do also, but these latter provide little heat. Check the label on your UV fluorescent package carefully. Many of them will emit UV for only the first six months of the bulb's life. Old bulbs may light up, but will often provide none of the UV your box turtles need to stay healthy.

Although UV cannot hurt your turtles, and is probably very beneficial, there is now evidence that it is not an absolute necessity for raising healthy box turtles. Ample heat combined with D3 and calcium additives seem sufficient.

Box turtles will be most comfortable if they have a hiding place. This can be a cardboard box with an entry hole, arced cork bark, or a commercially available hide box (these are simply called "hides" in the pet trade). However, even if a hide box is provided, some specimens may prefer to merely wedge themselves tightly into a corner each night. Small potted shrubs with nontoxic foliage can be used as decoration. However, most species of shrubs will require very bright light and a fair amount of humidity to survive.

## Outdoor Caging

Outdoor caging both decreases your workload and often provides a better environment for your box turtles. Outside pens can be made from boards set edgewise with the lower 2 or 3 inches (5 to 8 cm) set in narrow trenches. The boards should be at least 12 inches (30 cm) in width to create fencing that will keep your box turtles from roaming, and there should be a 4-inch (10-cm) overhang to guard against escape. We usually just nail strips of vinyl siding around the upper edge of the pen. It's light-weight and is easily screwed or nailed into place atop a 1-by-12-inch board (2.5 by 30 cm), and its natural floppiness makes it impossible for a box turtle's claws to get enough purchase to clamber over it.

Although most species of box turtles will be satisfied with just a shallow drinking and soaking dish, both the Malayan and the Chinese three-striped box turtles will require swimming facilities. For these, plan on a larger outdoors enclosure, one that includes space for the pool and space for wandering. A children's wading pool (or similar receptacle) can be sunk nearly to its rim in the ground. Ramps permitting easy access to and from the water must be added. The water can be cleaned by draining the pool with a small pump and refilling it with a garden hose.

Care must be taken that predators—dogs, cats, raccoons, opossums, crows, magpies, and other unwanted species—cannot access your turtle's cage. Even small burrowing mammals such as moles and mice can make themselves unwanted by consuming box turtle eggs and hatchlings before they leave the nest. Fire ants can be persistent and deadly. Where these insects occur, their presence in an outside cage must be continuously guarded against.

The length of time during the day/year that your turtles can be kept outside will be determined by both the ambient outside temperature and the species and subspecies of box turtle involved. As may be expected, species from the northerly temperate regions can withstand cooler tempera-

This is a portrait of a large female Chinese three-striped box turtle, *Cuora trifasciata*.

This is an alert male eastern box turtle, *Terrapene c. carolina*.

tures for a longer period than can tropical forms.

In northern Florida we are able to keep all races of eastern box turtle, as well as the Asian yellow-rimmed box turtle and Chinese three-striped box turtle, outside throughout the year. We have added a small heated house to their pen. All our box turtles become quite inactive during the winter months. They may occasionally thermoregulate in the brilliant sunlight by day, but more often remain in shallow depressions they have dug, sometimes for many days on end. During extended periods of very cold winter weather, the turtles often eventually gather inside their heated house. They become used to this lamp-heated haven during the months of winter, and even after we turn the electricity off in midspring, it takes them many weeks to once again scatter around their enclosure. We use red or blue heat lamps to heat the house. Neither of these colors seem to disturb the box turtles' circadian rhythms and breeding cycles in the slightest.

Box turtles are not agile and, during the normal course of their daily activities, one may overturn. On soft ground it is often difficult for the turtle to right itself. If the substrate on which they are lying won't provide a proper foothold, it can be impossible for the overturned turtle to right itself. If this occurs in the full sunlight, or beneath a heat lamp, it is possible that the turtle may overheat and die. Although there is no fail-safe method to prevent this, you *must* take every precaution possible. Take stock of your caging, "redecorate" as prudent, provide nonslick flooring, and check the well-being of your box turtles daily.

If you feed the box turtles in one place and at a particular time, the creatures will often gather daily in anticipation of their meal.

In some areas of the country cinder block walls are commonly placed around yards and gardens. These are ideal for restraining box turtles and need no additional preparation at all.

Although they are collectively called Malayan box turtles and designated scientifically as *Cuora amboinensis,* there may be more than one species involved. Note the pinkish color on this shell.

Adult desert box turtles, *Terrapene ornata luteola,* are usually busily patterned.

The pretty Chinese box turtle, *Cuora (Cistoclemmys) flavomarginata,* is popular among hobbyists.

# Feeding and Watering Your Box Turtle

## Watering

It is important that your box turtle(s) be provided with clean water at all times. A suitable water dish must be shallow, easy to drink from, and easily accessed (and egressed) if your turtle happens to want to crawl in and soak. During the hot days of summer the turtles may spend considerable time just sitting complacently in an inch or so of clean water. Water receptacles must have smooth sides that will not abrade the turtle's plastron as it climbs in and out, and they must be large enough to allow the turtle to right itself if it happens to accidentally turn over while entering or exiting. Box turtles may choose to defecate in their water supply, so daily cleaning should become your routine. The receptacle can be sterilized with a weak bleach solution (1 part bleach to 10 parts water), then thoroughly rinsed.

## Feeding

A healthful diet is a keynote to long-term success with your box turtles. A healthful diet will include a wide variety of plant and animals materials,

and your box turtle should not be allowed to eat only one or two particular favorites from this.

Box turtles will eat all manner of fruits, dark lettuces (such as romaine and escarole), and collard and dandelion leaves and blossoms, as well as worms, slugs, snails, insects, puppy chow, canned dog foods, and pelletized chow formulated for trout, catfish, and cats. Many of the commercial turtle foods now available are excellent supplements.

Eastern and Asian box turtles are particularly fond of earthworms.

Western and Mexican box turtles are often preferentially insectivorous.

An occasional prekilled pinky mouse will usually be eagerly accepted by all species and subspecies of box turtles.

This is a portrait of a dark-shelled Malayan box turtle, *Cuora amboinensis*.

Many keeled box turtles, *Pyxidea mouhoti,* have rich mahogany color on the sides of the carapace.

Although box turtles are almost always ready to eat, their intake of food should be moderated. Turtles are ectotherms, and their body functions are more rapid when the turtles are warm than when they are cool. When they become too cold, digestion can stop and the food putrefies in the gut, causing distress or even the death of the turtle or tortoise. (See the cautionary note about preparing your box turtle for hibernation, page 40.)

Your box turtle will be most comfortable at a body temperature from 78 to 90°F (25.6 to 32.2°C). It will eat a great deal of food and best metabolize when within this temperature range. On cool days, if the sun is shining, the turtle will bask to elevate its body temperature to within the desired range. On hot days the turtle will seek the cooling protection of the shade or may soak in its shaded water receptacle.

Deprived in captivity of space for normal activity, box turtles can become unhealthily obese. A telltale sign of obesity will be your box turtle's inability to close its plastron

fully. Adjust the diet and allow your turtle more exercise if it shows signs of being overweight.

A box turtle that is hungry often seems to be restless, and moves about its enclosure, nosing at objects in its way. Unfortunately, a chelonian that has gone without proper food for too long becomes weakened and apathetic; food that is offered too late may not be eaten, even when placed in full view.

Generally, if a food-deprived eastern or Asian box turtle has even a marginal remaining interest in food, a wriggling nightcrawler or earthworm will trigger a feeding response. The box turtle will almost jump on the worm in its haste to feed! Western box turtles are less enthusiastic about worms, but are usually instantaneously interested in—are you ready for this?—dung beetles (oh, yes, and crickets and locusts). Once the turtle is feeding, it can be weaned over to a broader-spectrum diet. Treats of worms and crickets will always be appreciated.

Vitamin and mineral supplements are suggested dietary additives, especially for box turtles kept indoors. An insufficient amount of vitamins A and D3 and calcium can eventually lead to health problems for your box turtle. Supplementation is especially important in fast-growing hatchlings and juveniles and in ovulating females, all of which are actively metabolizing calcium.

For all reptiles, a diet with the correct calcium-to-phosphorus balance is important to maintain bone integrity. If the reptile does not receive enough calcium in its diet to maintain the correct level in the blood, the needed calcium is taken from the bones. The bones (and shell) are softened and muscles weaken; the syndrome is termed metabolic bone disease, or MBD.

To guard against MBD avoid feeding a great amount of food that is high in phosphorus and low in calcium. The ideal ratio is 2:1 (calcium:phosphorus). Supply high phosphorus–low calcium fruits such as grapes and bananas as only an occasional treat. Foods containing oxalic acid are another problem. The oxalic acid (such as found in spinach) combines with calcium to form a dangerous insoluble salt, calcium oxalate. This will accumulate in the kidneys and can eventually be fatal.

Vitamin D3 assists in the proper metabolization of calcium. The proper utilization of D3-calcium is activated by ultraviolet lighting (UV-B specifically—see also the role of ultraviolet lighting on page 23). Most calcium additives designed for reptile consumption now contain D3. Improper metabolization of calcium or actual lack of calcium in the diet can result in soft bones and shell.

Hatchling eastern box turtles, *Terrapene c. carolina*, are brown with light carapacial spots.

Make certain that the diet you provide fulfills your chelonian's needs from the start. Should your box turtle develop a calcium deficiency, consult your reptile veterinarian. Calcium-D3 injections are often able to stabilize or actually reverse the deterioration and a better, more balanced diet will help prevent reccurrence.

If allowed to do so, box turtles can quickly develop unhealthful dietary habits. Do not give them the opportunity. Offer your box turtle a balanced, healthful diet that provides the vitamins and mineral your turtle needs to assure its full life span.

The yellow-headed box turtle, *Cuora aurocapitata*, is no longer seen with regularity in the pet trade.

# Health

When properly acclimated, kept in suitable cages, and fed properly, box turtles are among the hardiest of species. Like any living creature, however, they may occasionally develop a health problem that requires assessment or treatment by a reptile-qualified veterinarian. Because not all veterinarians are qualified to treat reptiles, nor do all choose to do so, you should find an animal care specialist before his or her services are actually needed.

And with that said, let's look at a few of the problems you may encounter.

Many keepers of turtles and tortoises can, like us, remember when baby turtles were offered for sale on the countertops of almost every variety store in America. Now turtles less than 4 inches (10 cm) in length can be sold only to researchers.

Why is this so and how did it come to be?

Well, certainly from the humane standpoint some changes were needed. But it was not the ethics of humane treatment that brought about the cessation of baby turtle sales. Rather, it was concern about the possible spread of a bacterial disease—salmonellosis (often just referred to by the generic name of the bacterium—salmonella).

The fallacy, of course, is that though the turtles may not fit easily in the mouth, fingers do. If salmonella are present, unwashed hands can easily transmit the bacteria to the mouth.

Thus, the bottom line here is to caution both adults and children: Turtles *can* carry diseases that are transmissible to humans, and you may inadvertently introduce pathogens to your pets if you handle them or offer them food without first washing your hands. If you wash your hands both before and after handling any pet turtles or tortoises, you will help protect both your pets and yourselves.

This is a beautifully marked Indochinese box turtle, *Cuora (Cistoclemmys) galbinifrons.*

Today, additional laws affecting the availability of turtles and tortoises in the pet trade have also been enacted. Because of plummeting populations (caused by habitat and nest destruction and collecting for pet, food, and research markets), many states now fully or partially protect all (or some) indigenous turtle species. Endangered species regulations, on state, federal, and international levels, offer an even greater level of protection to some species. Importation restrictions limit the availability of many foreign turtle species once coveted by American hobbyists.

But despite all the laws and regulations, people continue to keep turtles and tortoises, baby and otherwise. Many people, such as Patti and I, are breeders of both common and unusual taxa. Baby turtles are found by anglers who take them home to their children, kids pick up box and wood turtles on woodland pathways, and there are reptile dealers who can supply a vast number of species. Specialty clubs, catering to cheloniophiles (turtle enthusiasts) are present in many large cities.

Thus, if you want a turtle, you can get a turtle—and that many people not only do want a turtle, but also want to know more about them, is shown by the many health questions Patti and I field.

# Swollen Eyes and Peeling Skin

Vitamin A deficiency: Symptoms of acute vitamin A deficiency include swollen eyelids (and vision problems) and flaking, peeling, and (often) bloody skin patches. Although acute vitamin A deficiency is not often encountered, it occurs most commonly in rapidly growing hatchling and juvenile specimens that have had a very limited diet or that have had their (usually incorrect) diets supplemented with only D3-calcium additives.

Injectable vitamin A may reverse the problem, and a better, more balanced diet and multivitamins (rather than just D3) will prevent its recurrence.

# Swollen Eyelids

Several things other than vitamin A deficiency can cause swollen eyelids and impaired vision in turtles and tortoises. Among other reasons are insufficient humidity, old age, advanced systemic disease, and improper diet. A treatment of topical and/or systemic antibiotics is mandatory. Consult your veterinarian.

# Obesity

Obesity is as dangerous to turtles and tortoises as to any other animals. In cases of gross obesity, the functions of the liver and other organs are impaired. Correcting the diet in both quality and quantity is recommended.

# Respiratory Ailments

Clogged or runny nostrils, gasping with open mouth and wheezing, excessive mucus in the nose and mouth, and bubbling or foaming at the nose and/or mouth indicate serious respiratory problems. The causes can be numerous and alone or in combination. Respiratories, as they are familiarly called, can be lingering or rapidly fatal. Antibiotic treatment is mandatory but may differ according to the causative agent. Make your pet comfortable by making sure that its cage is warm enough, or that the turtle is under the hot spot, and consult your veterinarian immediately!

## Ear Infections

Ear infections are usually abscesses, resulting from overheating and a humidity too low for the species involved. They are not uncommon in terrestrial chelonians, and are quite common in box turtles. We have seen abscesses more rarely on aquatic turtles; poor water quality is most usually the cause in these cases.

Reptilian abscesses do not respond positively to systemic

Adult male ornate box turtles, *Terrapene o. ornata,* often have red eyes and greenish cheeks.

This is the hinged plastron of a Malayan box turtle, *Cuora amboinensis*.

treatments. The abscesses should be surgically removed by a veterinarian. Once the caseous material is removed, the site must be cleaned and bandaged daily. The flushing and dressing is often a simple matter that can be performed at home, but on strong chelonians that remain withdrawn for long periods, veterinary help may continue to be needed.

surrounding the trachea, the chelonian may suffocate. In all cases consult your veterinarian.

## Mouth Infections

Mouth infections may vary from abscesses to acute infectious stomatitis (literally an infection of the stoma [mouth]; also called mouthrot). Determining what antibiotic to use against the pathogen will require sensitivity tests. Stomatitis can be fatal, because it can quickly progress from tissue to bone structure. If it progresses to the tissues

## Shell Breaks/ Injuries

Depending on the severity of a shell break or injury, taping the shell together (for minor injuries) or flushing the area with antibiotic

Plain even when adult, hatchling three-toed box turtles, *Terrapene carolina triunguis* (such as this example) have few identifying features.

Hatchling ornate box turtles, *Terrapene o. ornata,* are flatter and marked less precisely than the adults.

This is an alert juvenile Chinese box turtle, *Cuora (Cistoclemmys) flavomarginata.*

Like their American counterparts, the babies of most Asian box turtles are less highly domed than the adults. This is a hatchling Chinese box turtle, *Cuora (Cistoclemmys) flavomarginata.*

treatment and debridement of fragmented shell pieces will be necessary. Fiberglass reconstruction may also be an option. Consult your veterinarian immediately.

## Ectoparasites (Ticks and Bot Fly Larvae)

Many terrestrial chelonians collected from the wild may have from one to many ticks attached. These may be removed after they have been relaxed with a drop of rubbing alcohol or mineral oil by grasping them firmly and pulling gently. One of the commercially available tick-removal tweezers may make it easier to remove these firm-mouthed arthropods. Be certain the embedded mouth parts are removed.

Certain parasitic flies may lay their eggs on the soft areas of a chelonian's skin. The larvae hatch and burrow beneath the skin. These should be surgically removed by a veterinarian

as soon as they are noticed. Bathe the incised area with antiseptics.

## Endoparasites

Over the course of their lives, many chelonians—even those that are captive-bred and hatched—may be found to have internal parasites. An occasional fecal float and/or mucus swab can determine whether parasites are present. If present, these parasites must be properly identified to be effectively purged. Because of the complexities of identification of endoparasites and the necessity to accurately weigh specimens to be treated and measure purge dosages, the eradication of internal parasites is best left to a qualified reptile veterinarian.

## Other Maladies

Other maladies, from arthritic problems and broken bones to complex infections, are known to afflict chelonians. Veterinary consultation, assessment, and treatment is necessary for most.

# Breeding Your Box Turtle

As box turtle populations around the world dwindle in number, it becomes ever more important that our captive populations of them become self-sustaining. Although herpetoculturists have bred many species, other species, such as the beautiful Indo-chinese box turtle, continue to defy our efforts to breed them in captivity.

In the wild, the breeding sequences of box turtles are, as are those of all other reptiles, triggered by external stimuli. To breed successfully and consistently in captivity, at least some of these stimuli need to be duplicated. Photoperiods (day length versus night length), seasonal weather changes (either the annual progression of cold to warm of the temperate regions, or merely the change from dry to rainy of the equatorial regions), changing humidity, changing barometric pressure, rainfall, and hibernation (when applicable), are among the external stimuli involved. Most box turtles are Northern Hemisphere species that utilize all of the environmental cues. Barometric pressure changes will be noticed by a box turtle even if it is kept indoors, but such factors as rainfall, photoperiods, and temperature changes will necessarily be up to you.

Box turtles (all turtles, for that matter) reproduce by means of eggs. The first clutch of eggs may be laid in three to six weeks after mating. Most female box turtles nest two or three (sometimes more) times each season at about three-week intervals, depositing one to eight eggs per clutch. The females are capable of "sperm storage," and may lay fertile eggs for several years after a single mating.

How long it takes for the eggs to hatch is dictated by nest temperature and (probably) humidity. In other words, the egg responds to environmental conditions and may slow its development so that hatching occurs when conditions are optimal for the survival of the young. Excessive heat, cold, moisture, or dryness may cause the temporary slowing of embryonic development (diapause). Extremes may kill or deform the embryo. In the

This pair of three-toed box turtles, *Terrapene carolina triunguis,* is breeding.

Subadult three-toed box turtles, *Terrapene carolina triunguis,* are often very rounded and of a dark color.

Carl May photographed this Gulf Coast box turtle, *Terrapene carolina major,* while it was hatching.

wild the hatchlings usually emerge during periods of optimal weather, but some embryos may overwinter in the nest before finishing development and emerging.

In keeping with the small size of an adult female box turtle, an average clutch of box turtle eggs is usually few in number. Although up to eight eggs have been recorded (eastern box turtle, ornate box turtle) the more usual number is from three to five. Asian keeled box turtles have been known to produce up to five eggs, but the other Asian species—those of the genus *Cuora*—produce only one or two eggs in each clutch.

How do the opposite sexes find each other in the wild? Certainly box turtles are endowed with excellent visual acuity and are often present in suitable habitats in fair numbers. As a result, they may randomly sight one another or just happen across one another. However, during periods of female reproductive receptivity,

encounters seem to be a little more than just random.

It is known that most reptiles produce pheromones, scented hormones relating to reproduction. Since the glands in which the pheromones are produced enlarge during periods of reproductive activity, pheromone output is probably greatest at that time. Pheromones are species specific, advertising the receptivity of a female only to the males of their own species. During the breeding season male box turtles seem to easily find prospective mates and may even trail them for long distances, so it seems likely that pheromone production is a major player in the mating game.

Some species of box turtles indulge in a cursory courtship prior to mating, whereas other species do not. The courtship of the semiaquatic box turtles often occurs in the water. The males of the various races of eastern box turtle circle their prospective mates, nipping at the feet, legs, head, neck, and anterior of the shell of the females. The males of the western box turtles largely dispense with courtship, merely nudging the rear of the female's shell, then mounting and breeding her. The courtship of the males of the various Asian box turtles is quite rough, with the female being first immobilized by bites to her anterior, then mounted and bred.

The males of the high-domed species (eastern and western box turtles, yellow-margined box turtle, Indochinese box turtle) retain their breeding position by clinging with their hind claws to the skin at the apex of the female's rear legs or to the posterior rim of the female's shell. To help facilitate this the male western box turtles have developed a jointed innermost toe. The females also help the males retain position.

Males of some of the less highly domed species hold the female with all four feet.

Captive box turtles of all kinds must be provided a suitable nesting area. Those that are well acclimated to captivity will most often nest as naturally as they would in the wild. Most females dig a well-defined nest that is just about as deep as the turtles are able to reach with their hind feet. However, some of the Asian species dig only a shallow nest that may barely hold the two eggs. Box turtles prefer soil that is just damp enough to retain its integrity as the nesting chamber is dug. Collapsing sides or insufficient depth of nesting medium may compel the female to temporarily discontinue her nesting attempts.

As she digs, the female box turtle will moisten the soil with water from her bladder. As the eggs are laid, the female reaches down into the nest with a hind foot and positions each egg. The descent of the dropping eggs may be slowed somewhat by the expulsion of a thick, viscous fluid from the female's vent. Once the laying is completed, the female box turtle covers the nest and methodically tamps down the covering dirt.

Depending on the time of year, the rainfall, and the species of turtle that laid them, after the female has laid and covered her clutch, we may remove the eggs and incubate them artificially. We carefully place the eggs in the position in which they lay in the nest in small plastic containers half filled with dampened vermiculite. These are then put into the incubator.

A female Florida box turtle, *Terrapene carolina bauri,* prepares (left) and fills a nest after egg deposition.

# Making Your Own Incubator

Materials needed for one incubator:

1 wafer thermostat/heater (obtainable from feed stores; these are commonly used in incubators for chicks)

1 thermometer

1 Styrofoam cooler with thick sides (a fish-shipping box is ideal)

1 heat tape or hanging heating coil

1 electrical cord and wall plug

1 heavy hardware cloth bent into a shelf to hold egg containers an inch or two above the coiled heat tape

Your goal is to wire the thermostat between the heat tape and the electrical cord, in order to regulate the amount of heat produced by the heat tape.

Cut the electrical cord off the heat tape, leaving about 18 inches (45 cm) of the cord on the heat tape. Make a hole through the side of the Styrofoam box, about 5 inches (12 cm) below the top edge. Pull the electrical cord through the hole, leaving the plug end outside (don't plug it in just yet!). Strip off about a half inch (1 cm) of the insulation from the wiring at the cut end, and separate the two wires for a few inches.

Coil the heat tape loosely in the bottom of the Styrofoam box, making sure that it doesn't cross over itself at any point. Coil the tape so the recently cut end is near the electrical cord. Strip off about a half an inch of the insulation from the end of the wiring, and separate the two wires for a few inches.

Using one of the wire nuts, connect one of the red wires of the thermostat to one of the electrical wires of the heat tape. Use a second nut to connect the second red wire of the thermostat to one of the wires of the electrical cord. The third nut is used to connect the second wire of the electrical cord to the second wire of the heat tape (in effect, re-establishing part of the original wiring between the heat tape and its electrical cord.)

That's all there is to it. Put the lid on the cooler, and plug in the thermostat/heater. Wait half an hour and check the temperature. The L-shaped pin on the top of the thermostat is the rheostat; turn it to increase or decrease the temperature inside your new incubator. You want the inside to be 80–86°F (27–30°C).

Once you have the temperature regulated, add your hardware cloth "shelf," and put the container of eggs atop the shelf. Close the egg container.

Check the temperature daily and add a little water to the incubating medium if it gets dry (it should stay damp enough to stick together when you stick your finger into it, or when you push it into a little heap with your finger). Take care to add the water to the medium, *not* onto the eggs. The preferred humidity is 100 percent. Placing an open deli container, half filled with water, onto the hardware cloth shelf will also help maintain the humidity.

This Florida box turtle, *Terrapene carolina bauri,* was hatching after 66 days of incubation.

Many herpetoculturists feel that it is very important that the eggs *not* be rotated on either longitudinal axis when they are removed. Although we do not feel that this is absolutely essential, neither do we tempt fate. To help us with egg orientation, we pencil a small "X" on the top of each egg before it is moved. Once laid, turtle eggs, unlike bird eggs, do not require turning during incubation, and at some points in the incubation, turning the egg may be fatal to the developing embryo.

If you allow the eggs of your box turtle to incubate naturally, be certain that they are protected from predators. Crows, magpies, and blue jays will watch a nesting female and steal the eggs as they are laid. These birds and mammalian predators will also dig the eggs from the nests and eat them, or eat newly hatched babies. Fire ants have become a major predator of hatching turtles, at times eating the hatchlings in the nest.

Box turtle eggs are elongate and have a pliable shell. If given the opportunity, most female box turtles will dig a nesting chamber. Should they happen to scatter the eggs in the terrarium, remove them carefully (trying to retain the position in which they are lying) from the terrarium and place them, half buried in the chosen incubation medium, in the incubator. We use dampened vermiculite, stirring in 1 part water to 4 parts vermiculite until the medium clumps together. Then we hand-squeeze out as much water as possible and place the medium in a plastic container with a lid.

Infertile eggs may discolor and collapse. If you are certain the eggs are infertile, they may be removed and discarded. Embryo death may occasionally occur during incubation or, rarely, even as the full-term young are trying to break from their eggs.

At the end of the incubation period—which may vary (by species and incubation temperature) from about 65 to more than 90 days—hatching will occur. Assisted by some biodegrading of the shell, the hatchlings cut their way free of the egg with an egg tooth (this tooth drops off in a few days). It may take a day or longer for the hatchling to finally emerge from the egg. When they emerge from their eggs, hatchling chelonians usually have large umbilical egg sacs. These are absorbed over a period of time ranging from a few hours to about two days. The hatchlings will not need, or even want, to feed until the egg sac has been fully used.

The hatchlings should be moved to a small terrarium and offered food, a sunning spot, an area of seclusion (damp sphagnum moss in which they can burrow is ideal), and water.

Despite having a huge egg sac, this hatchling Florida box turtle, *Terrapene carolina bauri,* emerged quickly from the egg. The sac was absorbed within 24 hours.

Like all hatchling American box turtles, those of the Florida box turtle, *Terrapene carolina bauri,* are very different from the adults.

Hatchling box turtles are delicate and, because of the yolk sac, clumsy. Take care that the babies are not on a substrate sufficiently abrasive to rupture the yolk sac. We often keep ours on dampened paper towels or on dampened sphagnum moss inside their own terrarium until the yolk sac has been absorbed. We provide all hatchlings with an even warmth for the first few weeks of their lives.

If you take the hatchlings outside, remember that predators come in many forms. Jays, crows, and grackles all eagerly eat baby turtles. Fire ants (and other ants) can quickly find those hatchlings on the ground. Cats, dogs, opossums, mice, rats, and raccoons are all dangerous to your babies. Sunlight itself, usually a coveted ally in the breeding and raising of turtles, can become an adversary and quickly overheat an improperly situated container.

## Hibernation

The importance of providing a varying period of winter dormancy in the life expectancy of turtles physiologically adapted for hibernating is largely unknown. Certainly some box turtles from the northern temperate climes can be kept for decades, and even bred for a few years, without being hibernated. This has been amply proven by breeding successes with eastern box turtles kept in outside facilities in southern Florida. However, many breeders have reported a decline in the viability of eggs laid after a few years of nonhibernation by their turtles. Because there are no properly hibernated control

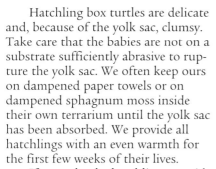

A clutch of three Florida box turtle eggs, *Terrapene carolina bauri,* (bottom near coin) incubates.

specimens available for comparison, it is unknown whether the nonhibernation or some other factor is at fault.

Certainly a period of hibernation—or at least brief periods of winter dormancy—is a natural occurrence for many box turtles. If you want to breed your box turtles more than once or twice, we suggest that you provide a similar period of cold temperatures, darkness, and turtle inactivity.

At our facility in northern Florida, eastern and three-toed box turtles are hibernated for a duration of 60–70 days in a converted refrigerator at a temperature of 40–45°F (13.1–16.1°C). An electrician changed the thermostat in the refrigerator for us; regular refrigerators get too cold, even with the installed thermostat set as warm as it will go. Southern species, such as yellow-margined and Florida box turtles, are merely left to their own devices in outside pens. During the passage of cold fronts these latter turtles burrow about the depth of their shell into the ground, usually against a bunch of grass or the roots of a shrub, and may remain there for several days at a time. Sometimes they are roused when we have several warm days in succession (especially if we turn on the lawn sprinklers in the enclosure for a few hours).

Both the cool-refrigerator and the outside-pen regimens seem to work well, and our various box turtles have successfully bred for many years without a break.

However, hibernation is not necessarily stress-free for chelonians, whether in the wild or in captivity. Death is far from a stranger at these times. If your box turtle is not in A-1 condition, do not hibernate it.

Your hibernation candidates must be heavy (but not overly fat), be parasite free, have no signs of respiratory distress, and be free of any other signs of illness or disease.

Once the basic very-good-health requirement has been met, stop feeding your box turtles for a few weeks before they enter hibernation. Your box turtle's gut must be empty of food before the animal is hibernated, and this won't happen overnight.

A chelonian's rate of digestion varies by temperature. Warm days and warm nights equal rapid digestion. Warm days and cool nights equal

Immature desert box turtles, *Terrapene ornata luteola,* are so secretive that they are not often seen in the wild.

This hatchling Florida box turtle, *Terrapene carolina bauri,* has more yellow than most.

This baby aquatic box turtle, *Terrapene coahuila,* was hatched in the captive-breeding program of Gladys Porter Zoo, Brownsville, TX.

slower digestion, and cool days and cool nights mean very slow digestion. Again, you must know your animal and your temperatures so you can stop feeding it from two weeks (warm areas) to four weeks (cool areas) before it is allowed to hibernate. An occasional soak in warm water may hasten defecation. Err on the side of safety. Continue to provide water throughout the prehibernation fast.

For those box turtles spending their hibernation period outdoors, consider adding some protection after the turtles have burrowed in. Many hobbyists in the northern United States add a cover of a foot or so of fallen leaves to the pen after the chelonians have dug in and entered dormancy. Make certain that your pets have not selected a part of the pen that is subject to flooding.

In temperate areas, some hobbyists hibernate their box turtles in root cellars or other such underground "steady temperature" storage areas. You want an area that will provide temperatures of 35–45°F (10.5–16.1°C). The box turtles may be hibernated in a large box of dried leaves and pine needles, or nonaromatic wood shavings. The best temperature inside the box or hibernaculum seems to be between 40–44°F (13.1–15.6°C). We use the vegetable bins in our converted refrigerator as a hibernaculum; a thermometer in the hibernaculum enables us to check the temperature.

At the end of the hibernation period, box turtles that are hibernating naturally will respond to the warmer temperatures, longer day length, and gentle, warm rains. They simply wake up and emerge for another season of activity. For those box turtles being held in artificial hibernations, return the ambient temperature of those being artificially hibernated to normal by placing the turtles and their hibernaculum at room temperature, and allow the turtles to awaken. All should be offered fresh food and water.

Captive box turtles, whether tropical or temperate in origin, can be induced to remain active year-round by maintaining long day lengths with electric bulbs and keeping the animals warm. That the turtles know something is amiss is often attested to by diminished appetites and inordinate lethargy during the months they would normally be hibernating/resting. Is this healthy for them in the long run? We simply don't know yet, but have seen no indications of ill effects.

Breeding turtles and watching your very own captive-bred and -hatched young grow and mature can be immensely satisfying, but it is also a lengthy endeavor that requires much thought and care.

# Glossary

**Aestivation:** A period of warm weather inactivity; often triggered by excessive heat or drought.

**Albino:** Lacking black pigment.

**Ambient temperature:** The temperature of the surrounding environment.

**Anterior:** Toward the front.

**Anus:** The external opening of the cloaca; the vent.

**Axilla:** The areas where the legs join the body.

**Bridge:** The "bridge of shell" between fore and rear limbs that connects the carapace and the plastron.

**Brumation:** The reptilian and amphibian equivalent of mammalian hibernation.

**Carapace:** The upper shell of a chelonian.

**Chelonian:** A turtle or tortoise.

**Chorioallantois:** The gas-permeable membranous layer inside the shell of a reptile egg.

**Cloaca:** The common chamber into which digestive, urinary, and reproductive systems empty and which itself opens exteriorly through the vent or anus.

**Deposition:** As used here, the laying of the eggs or birthing of young.

**Deposition site:** The nesting site.

**Dimorphic:** A difference in form, build, or coloration involving the same species; often sex-linked.

**Diurnal:** Active in the daytime.

**Ectothermic:** "Cold-blooded."

**Form:** An identifiable species or subspecies.

**Genus:** A taxonomic classification of a group of species having similar characteristics. The genus falls between the next higher designation of

Eastern box turtles, *Terrapene c. carolina,* are often found in grassy pastures.

Hatchling Gulf Coast box turtles, *Terrapene carolina major,* are very dark and sparingly marked.

This large and pretty eastern box turtle, *Terrapene c. carolina,* was photographed in a yard in Missouri.

This dark-colored eastern box turtle, *Terrapene c. carolina,* was seen in Kentucky.

"family" and the next lower designation of "species." Genera is the singular of genus. It is always capitalized when written.

**Hibernaculum:** Winter den. In the case of a box turtle, this may simply be a leaf or mulch-filled box, kept in the cool hibernation area.

**Hibernate:** Winter dormancy.

**Hinge:** The transverse cartilaginous connection that permits the plastron of box turtles to be movable.

**Hybrid:** Offspring resulting from the breeding of two species or two non-contiguous subspecies.

**Hydrate:** To restore body moisture by drinking or absorption.

*Pyxidea mouhoti* is commonly called the keeled box turtle. This is a hatchling.

**Intergrade:** Offspring resulting from the breeding of two contiguous subspecies.

**Keel:** A carapacial or plastral ridge (or ridges).

**Mandibles:** Jaws.

**Marginals:** The scales or scutes rimming the upper shell or plastron of a turtle

**Ontogenetic:** Age-related (color) changes.

**Photoperiod:** The daily/seasonally variable length of the hours of daylight.

**Plastron:** The bottom shell.

**Scute:** A plate on a turtle's shell.

**Species:** A group of similar creatures that produce viable young when breeding. The taxonomic designation that falls beneath genus and above subspecies. Abbreviation, "sp."

**Subspecies:** The subdivision of a species. A race that may differ slightly in color, size, scalation, or other criteria. Abbreviation, "ssp."

**Terrestrial:** Land-dwelling.

**Thermoregulate:** To regulate (body) temperature by choosing a warmer or cooler environment.

# Special Interest Groups

## Turtle and Tortoise Clubs

There are several turtle and tortoise clubs in major cities in North America and Europe. Most of the organizations produce informative newsletters and are actively trying to promote chelonian conservation and "cheloniocuture." All welcome inquiries and new members.

The Tortoise Trust
c/o Tortoise Trust USA
PMB #2929
Owadonna, MN 55060
*http://www.tortoisetrust.org*

The New York Turtle and Tortoise
Society
163 Amsterdam Ave., Ste. 465
New York, NY 10023
*http://nytts.org/index..html*

California Turtle and Tortoise Club
P.O. Box 7300
Van Nuys, CA 91409
*http://www.tortoise.org*

National Tortoise and Turtle Society
P.O. Box 66935
Phoenix, AZ 85082

San Diego Turtle and Tortoise Society
P.O. Box 519
Imperial Beach, CA 91933
*http://www.sdturtle.org/*

Box Turtle Coalition of the NE
P.O. Box 350
Port Monmouth, NJ 07758
*http://www.herpconservation.org/ btcne/*

## Professional Societies

Society for the Study of Amphibians
and Reptiles
Dept. of Zoology
Miami University
Oxford, OH 45056
*http://www.ukans.edu/˜ssar*

Fellow amateurs and professionals may also be found at the biology departments of museums, universities, high schools, and nature centers.

Herpetological societies exist in many larger cities. Check at pet stores or universities to learn whether one exists in your area.

Hobbyist magazines that publish articles on turtles and tortoises are

*Reptiles*
P.O. Box 6050
Mission Viejo, CA 92690
*http://animalnetwork.com/reptiles/ default.asp*

*Reptile and Amphibian Hobbyist*
211 W. Sylvania Ave.
Neptune City, NJ 07753
*http://www.tfh.com*

# Index

Bold page numbers indicate photographs.